NEW YORK CITY CONFIDENTIAL

HIDDEN GEMS LOVED BY LOCALS

WRITTEN BY TARAJIA MORRELL AND HANNAH FRISHBERG

JONGLEZ PUBLISHING

Travel guides

QUITE SIMPLY,
I WAS IN LOVE WITH NEW YORK.
I DO NOT MEAN “LOVE” IN ANY COLLOQUIAL WAY,
I MEAN THAT I WAS IN LOVE WITH THE CITY,
THE WAY YOU LOVE THE FIRST PERSON
WHO EVER TOUCHES YOU
AND YOU NEVER LOVE ANYONE QUITE
THAT WAY AGAIN.

JOAN DIDION

WHAT YOU WON'T FIND IN THIS GUIDE

- avocado toast
- Broadway recommendations
- places to take an Instagram photo (Be in the moment!)

WHAT YOU WILL FIND IN THIS GUIDE

- how to eat pizza like a New Yorker (Warning: it's controversial)
- fantastic speakeasies
- restaurants known only to true New Yorkers
- tips for spending perfect days in Harlem, Queens, or Williamsburg
- the best wellness spots in the city
- where to play tennis in a train station

Opening times often vary,
so we recommend checking them directly
on the website of the place you plan to visit.

SYMBOLS USED IN
NEW YORK CITY CONFIDENTIAL

Free

Less
than $20

$20
to $100

More
than $100

First come,
first served

Make
a reservation

So
New York!

Lovely
for couples

NEW YORK
MANHATTAN
QUEENS
BROOKLYN
GOVERNORS ISLAND
ROCKAWAYS

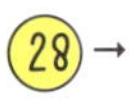

01. One of New York's finest hotels
02. Cocktails on the rooftop of historic skyscraper
03. Float away in an ancient bath
04. A museum in an elevator
05. The magic trio of Chinatown
06. A cinema unlike any other
07. The most "appetizing" restaurant in New York
08. Retro-quirky, Thai American diner
09. Broadway's most unexpected spa
10. Visit Donald Judd's creative world
11. Gift like a New Yorker
12. Iconic places, not secret. Just unmissable
13. One of New York's best speakeasies
14. The secret spot from where you can see New York's craziest building
15. An architectural cruise around Manhattan
16. Stargazing ... from the High Line
17. Experience an AI massage
18. Play tennis in a 107-year-old train station
19. Enjoy an aperitif in front of Ludwig Bemelmans' murals
20. A kosher deli hiding a cocktail bar
21. Have your bike blessed
22. A marvelous morning in Harlem
23. Enjoy classical music in the city's secret crypts
24. A secret Japanese bar hidden at the back of a bistro
25. Everlasting pizza party
26. Williamsburg punch list
27. A new-generation sauna
28. Not your average launderette
29. A bucolic waterway in the heart of the Bronx
30. How to conquer Queens
31. A wild experience
32. New York City's very own surf town

#01

ONE OF NEW YORK'S **FINEST HOTELS**

A stone's throw from Canal Street, Nine Orchard brings new life to the former Jarmulowsky Bank, a 1912 building transformed into a 113-room hotel. The magnificent renovation honors its neo-Renaissance heritage, right up to the small temple-like domed structure on the roof. The lobby feels pleasantly intimate at first, before the building reveals the spectacular grandeur of the former banking hall.

The rooms are all about light and height: sun-drenched and perched high above the bustle of the Lower East Side. The Design Suite is a particular favorite, with its balcony offering stunning views of the skyline through Corinthian-inspired columns.

Nine Orchard is as much a destination as a place to sleep. The Corner Bar bistro puts a fresh spin on American classics in a relaxed, convivial setting, whilst the Swan Room – a grand salon in the former tellers' hall – serves expertly crafted cocktails to the gentle sound of a piano.

NINE ORCHARD
9 ORCHARD STREET
NEW YORK, NY 10002

+212 804 9900

Instagram: @nineorchard
nineorchard.com

Restaurants :
cornerbarnyc.com
swanroomnyc.com

#02

COCKTAILS ON THE ROOFTOP OF HISTORIC SKYSCRAPER

When 70 Pine Street was completed in the financial district in 1932, its height (942 ft.) and 67 floors made it the third tallest building in the world. At the time, its uppermost floors were reserved exclusively for senior executives.

Today, the Overstory bar occupies the 64th floor of this listed landmark. With its backlit marble, brass counter, elegant furnishings, and area covering barely 603 sq. ft., the place is deliberately intimate. But the real draw is outside: from the rooftop, Manhattan unfolds in every direction. The view is so striking that the place feels as much like an observation deck as a cocktail bar. To reach the bar, take the lift from the red marble hall up to the Saga restaurant, then climb one floor higher up the stairs.

Beyond the (pricey) drinks, the concise menu offers oysters, white sturgeon caviar, and small barbecued lamb rolls.

OVERSTORY
70 PINE STREET (64TH FLOOR)
FINANCIAL DISTRICT
NEW YORK, NY 10005

Reservations are possible but not required

+1 (212) 339 3963
overstory-nyc.com
Instagram: @overstory

© AIRE ANCIENT BATHS

03

FLOAT AWAY **IN AN ANCIENT BATH**

Descending into the Aire Ancient Baths in Tribeca is like entering another dimension. Housed in a former textile factory building built in 1833 with stunning exposed beams and brick, the thermal pool room is dark and soothing, quiet and sensual. It's the perfect place to rejuvenate from the noise and bustle of the city (and pretend you're in 5th-century Rome), with amenities and treatments comparable to a 5-star hotel.

There are experiences tailored to couples (and indeed couples love to come here together), including a bath in Spanish Ribera del Duero red wine, but our preference is for scrubbing ourselves with sea salt and then floating in the soothing and serene salt water pool.

T.M.

AIRE ANCIENT BATHS
88 FRANKLIN STREET
NEW YORK, NY 10013

+1 (646) 878 6174

beaire.com
bookingnytribeca@beaire.com

#04

A MUSEUM **IN AN ELEVATOR**

Measuring barely 5 feet across, Mmuseumm is quite possibly New York's most unusual museum. It occupies a former freight lift at the end of a Lower Manhattan alleyway and opens only at weekends. But the heavy steel doors feature portholes and a phone number you can call for information about the curious objects lining the walls – making this the city's only 24-hour museum.

The attention to detail is impressive: white moldings, rich velvet, engraved brass plaques. There's even a café' (a small electric espresso machine) and a shop' (a 12-inch shelf with pencils bearing the museum's understated logo). The museum conventions are so carefully observed that it's hard to tell whether this is a clever parody or a serious institution.

MMUSEUMM
4 CORTLANDT ALLEY
NEW YORK, NY 10013

FREE

+1 (888) 763 8839
mmuseumm.com
info@mmuseumm.com

Open house on Saturdays and Sundays from 11am to 5pm
Exhibitions visible through portholes 24/7

Of course, it only works if the exhibitions are genuinely intriguing. Expect objects with hidden stories... That plain brown shoe? It's the one an Iraqi journalist threw at George W. Bush in 2008. The soap sculptures? Created by talented neo-Nazis whiling away time behind bars. And you'll probably see the world's only collection of Disney-branded bulletproof school backpacks.

According to Alex Kalman, one of the founders: These objects have passed through society and tell us something about human nature. We're here to look at society through them.'

Quirky, unconventional and wonderfully thought-provoking, Mmuseumm offers a unique lens on contemporary American life. Sure, it might be tiny, but it's absolutely unforgettable!

#05

THE MAGIC TRIO **OF CHINATOWN**

Oh, Chinatown, with your sidewalk offerings of squid and durian; your ageless characters spitting endlessly onto the pavement; your massage parlors, Chinese malls and, of course, restaurants. No visit to New York City is complete without a wander through these sticky streets, lived in for centuries by immigrants who flocked here on the wings of dreams of better lives. Chinatown offers velvet Chinese slippers, endless Asian tchotchkes, fake Gucci and Louis Vuitton bags, and some of the best food in the city. Royal Seafood, Golden Unicorn, Oriental Garden and Jin Fong are all great bets.

Our recommendation: have lunch at Dim Sum Go Go. The duck dumplings, the mushroom dumplings, the shrimp-and-chive dumplings, the turnip cake, and the honey-and-chive glazed nuts are absolutely to die for.

DIM SUM GO GO
5 EAST BROADWAY
(between CATHERINE STREET
& CHATHAM SQUARE), NEW YORK, NY 10038

+1 (212) 732 0797 | Instagram: @dimsumgogo | dimsumgogo.com

And since you're in the area, stop by the Mian Tian Hair Salon (170 Canal Street, 2nd floor): we love the "Shampoo/Blow/Style" package: a 10-min shoulder and neck massage, 5-min of massage and shampoo in the chair, then 10-min of massage and shampoo at the sink, followed by a blow-dry. Not bad for $15 to $25.

T.M.

MIAN TIAN SING HAIR SALON
170 CANAL STREET (2ND FLOOR)
NEW YORK, NY 10013

+1 (917) 353 5985	Instagram: @miantiansinghairsalon	miantiansingsalon.com

© MICHAEL CARNEVALE

Finally, head to Sunn's on Division Street. Behind a small green shopfront, you'll discover a welcoming wine bar, a handful of tables and a counter where chef Sunny Lee works her magic right in front of you. Don't miss the banchan – Korean small dishes traditionally served as accompaniments – perfect for sharing and sampling a bit of everything. Pair them with a natural wine (the wine list is curated with wine bar Parcelle) or a Korean beer, and finish on a sweet note with Sunny's famous sesame mochi cake.

SUNN'S
139 DIVISION STREET
NEW YORK, NY 10002

+ 1 (917) 540-0884

sunnsnyc.com
info@sunnsnyc.com

BOX OFFICE
UNCUT GEMS 12 2 30 PM
EYES WIDE SHUT 12 PM
LONG DAYS JOURNEY 3 30 PM
ATLANTICS 5 PM
PHANTOM THREAD 7 15

#06

A CINEMA **UNLIKE ANY OTHER**

Native New Yorker Alexander Olch had a dream: to create a sexy cinema that would reinvigorate the movie-going experience with a bit of Old Hollywood glamour. A visit to Metrograph is the manifestation of that dream.

On any given night, Metrograph screens films essential to the cinematic lexicon, whether instant contemporary classics or forever favorites; historic masters – Godard, Preminger, Wilder and Kubrick – to current game changers, like Noah Baumbach and Spike Jonze. Everything shown at Metrograph is chosen with purpose and projected on 35mm film, the artform's original medium (unless the movie was shot digitally).

Metrograph epitomizes what's great about New York – an ever-evolving city with characters who preserve culture to assure we have a textured future.

PRO TIP: Concession stand before the movie, Metrograph Commissary after.

T.M.

METROGRAPH
7 LUDLOW STREET
NEW YORK, NY 10002

+1 (212) 660 0312	Instagram: @metrograph	metrograph.com

LIVE
PRESENTS
EXIT

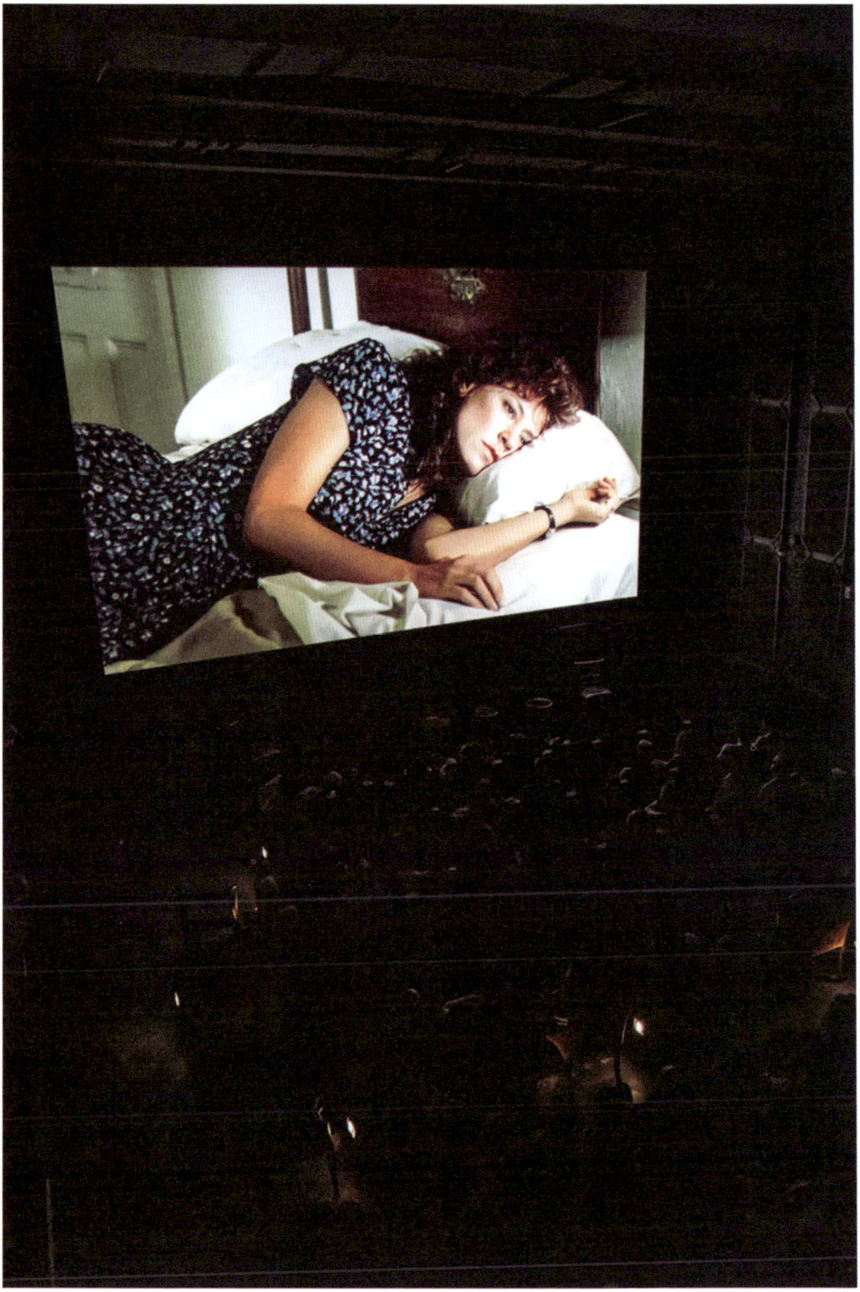

#07

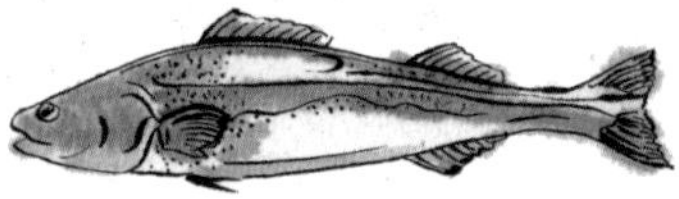

THE MOST "APPETIZING" RESTAURANT IN NEW YORK

In 1935, founder Joel Russ made a bold move: with no sons, three daughters and a thriving business, he made his daughters full partners and christened the family shop "Russ & Daughters" – the first American business to have "& Daughters" in its name.

Now, 106 years in, fourth-generation family members Josh Russ Tupper and Niki Russ Federman are *still* teaching New Yorkers (and many visitors) what "appetizing" means. They've expanded from the cherished storefront at 179 Houston to Russ & Daughters Cafe on Orchard Street (with outposts at the Brooklyn Navy Yard and Jewish Museum uptown too). The sublime cafe is adored for its housemade traditional Jewish cuisine with inventive flourishes. We prefer to skip the long lines at brunch in favor of weekday meals and romantic dinners of borscht, lox and, most importantly, Super Heebsters. T.M.

RUSS & DAUGHTERS CAFE
127 ORCHARD STREET
NEW YORK, NY 10002

+1 (212) 475 4880 ext. 2
russanddaughterscafe.com
Instagram: @russanddaughters

Shop: 179 E Houston Street
russanddaughters.com

SWEET
NOSHES
SOUPS
PLATTERS
RUS
NOSHES
SWEET

GHTERS
PLATTERS
EGGS
NOSHES
BOARDS
SOUPS
SWEET

- JOSH RUSS TUPPER & NIKI RUSS FEDERMAN -

FOURTH-GENERATION OWNERS OF RUSS & DAUGHTERS, THE FIRST BUSINESS IN AMERICA TO ADD "& DAUGHTERS" TO ITS NAME

You say your food category is "appetizing". But what does that mean?

NIKI: "Appetizing" is literally a taste of New York. It's a tradition that started with Jewish immigrants who landed here; it stayed in New York. The word got lost, but we've worked hard to reintroduce it; it's specific to New York.

JOSH: Appetizing is the sister food tradition to delicatessen. Deli is meat, and appetizing is dairy and cured and smoked fish. Appetizing is the food you put on a bagel!

At 106 years old, Russ & Daughters is an indelible institution, but maintaining a successful family-owned business in NYC is so hard. Was there ever a moment when you wondered if you wouldn't make it?

J: There's always that moment. There's always a curveball. Particularly when we committed to opening a restaurant when we didn't know anything about opening a restaurant!

N: Failing is not an option. There's the weight of responsibility of previous generations and our customers – New Yorkers. We didn't want to be the generation to mess it up. But we just keep looking back to that store on East Houston Street as the reference point for everything we do. We grow from there, so it's authentic and makes sense.

J: It's the long game.

Neither of you planned to go into the family business. Why did you?

N: I grew up appreciating that there was something very special happening in that store. Wherever I went in the world, if Russ & Daughters came up in conversation, the person's face lit up and they'd tell me their story about why Russ & Daughters is important to them. To feel the emotional impact that this place has on people, I realized it was something rare and that I wanted to continue that legacy.

What place or experience evokes the soul of New York for you?

J: The Freemans bar from 2003 to 2006, 6pm on Wednesdays, when Yana was bartending.

N: Jeremiah Stone and Fabian von Hauske, the chefs from Contra and Wildair across Orchard Street. Their trajectory here in this neighborhood, their success, what New York is to them, the potential for people to live out their dreams. The New York Story. T.M.

#08

RETRO-QUIRKY, **THAI AMERICAN DINER**

Our pulse quickens when we arrive and hear the retro Thai soundtrack.

When former fine dining chef couple Ann Redding and Matt Danzer opened Uncle Boons, their Michelin-starred restaurant inspired by the traditional Thai recipes of Redding's roots, they hoped it would be a success, but nothing could have prepared them for the deserved devotion of Boons' fans. Uncle Boons closed during Covid, but the flock has migrated down the street to their new all-day spot, Thai Diner.

Folks line up outside for a chance to nosh on fried chicken laab, spicy chopped chicken liver, massaman neuh and khao soi, all eaten with beer slushies, fun wine and cocktails in a quirky, merry atmosphere. It's a winning combination to be finished off with a Thai Coconut Sundae. T.M.

THAI DINER
186 MOTT STREET
NEW YORK, NY 10012

+1 (646) 850 9480 | Instagram: @thaidiner | thaidiner.com

© ALEX MUCCILLI

- ADAM PLATT -

Adam Platt is *New York Magazine*'s restaurant critic and for two decades has been sharing the trials, tribulations and delights of dining in our city and the merits of our food culture. Platt recently released *The Book of Eating*, a memoir about growing up in Hong Kong, Tokyo and France, and eventually becoming our most sardonic and amusing critic.

What do you think about our food-obsessed city?

In New York, there's an old dining culture, and you discover quickly that going out to restaurants is not just done occasionally but all the time. The family-togetherness meal is often something done in a restaurant. New Yorkers have this innate questing desire to discover and go to places, old and new, in a variety of different styles. New York has always been obsessed with what's in fashion, being in the know ... not just the best new French restaurant, but the most prosaic thing – the best pizza, ramen, burger – as the end of fine dining and beginning of millennial chef culture. What's been in fashion in terms of food for the last 15 to 20 years is the stuff that chefs are obsessed with: ingredients, technique, simplicity, innards, whatever the hell.

The variety is a reflection of the tapestry of New York

What makes New York a unique eating destination?

It's the combination of the three key things that make New York unique: the depth of dining culture; the variety of styles; and the close proximity and busyness that's the essence of life here. The depth of dining culture exists in Tokyo and Paris and any Italian city, but they don't have the variety. In LA you have great variety, but you don't have the dining culture. Here, it may not be the best Chinese, Malaysian or Mexican food in the world, but there are few places in the world where you can take a journey from borough to borough and taste the entire world. New York is the one place where you can often literally stay in one neighborhood and the world will come to you.

What's New York's terroir?

New York is a meat and potatoes town. The terroir of New York dining is an oyster and a piece of steak. The pizza slice, knish, bagel or hot dog, it's something that you do on the fly. It's something that's portable, something that meshes with the frenetic busyness of the city. Our versions are durable to survive the rigors of a New York day on the move; relatively cheap and reliably delicious with primary flavors and umami, stuff that cuts through the chaos.

What would you say is an iconic New York dish or dining experience?

My answer has always been the Grand Central Oyster Bar because it's in this nexus of movement and travel but everyone's moving and going somewhere, and oysters are our terroir food, but it's gotten so bad lately. Le Bernardin is a great neighborhood restaurant. Like all great New York restaurants, they function as neighborhood restaurants. It's the neighborhood restaurant for the midtown power older crowd. Run by a family. Chef is there – he's from somewhere else but he's indisputably a New York chef, who stays at his restaurant. You can't go there and not feel a sense of the grandeur of the city. If you want to feel the grandeur of New York, go to a late lunch at Le Bernardin.

T.M.

#09

BROADWAY'S MOST **UNEXPECTED SPA**

Nothing prepares you for what's on the fourth floor of this SoHo building. Spencer's grand salon looks like a collector's private apartment, but it's actually a cutting-edge spa that throws away the typical spa playbook.

After a few moments in a comfortable armchair observing the sculptures, ornaments and antique books on the coffee table, a therapist will lead you through a discreet entrance at the back of the salon and invite you to remove your shoes. Rather than the usual flimsy disposable slippers, you'll choose from a selection of color-coded socks – a stylish solution that maintains impeccable hygiene.

The treatment rooms lie hidden behind white linen curtains, arranged one after another down a corridor. Treatments include body massages – deep tissue, hot stone, gua sha – and facials with microcurrent technology to smooth fine lines and wrinkles. Best of all? The prices are remarkably reasonable for Manhattan.

SPENCER'S
550 BROADWAY (4TH FLOOR)
NEW YORK, NY 10012

One hour massage for non-members: $199

spencers.spa
Instagram: @spencers.spa

SPENCERS.SPA
RELAX.NYC
SNOWDON
The Paris Review
ABSTRACTION-GEOMETRY-PAINTING

#10

GIFT LIKE **A NEW YORKER**

Paula Rubenstein has a knack for finding gems, one-of-a-kind treasures that a less savvy scavenger might overlook, so luckily for us, she does the searching. Her eponymous Chrystie Street shop is a cave of wonders where one can hunt for antiques – paintings, textiles, furniture, books and curiosities – that tell stories with their pretty patina.

John Derian Company on 2nd Street is a one-stop shop for New Yorkers in search of the perfect gift. Derian carries the cult French ceramics line Astier de Villatte and represents artist Hugo Guinness, whose whimsical prints are collected by fashionable locals.

PAULA RUBENSTEIN
195 CHRYSTIE STREET
NEW YORK, NY 10002

+1 (212) 966 8954 | Instagram: @paularubenstein | paularubenstein.com

OGGI
EPOCA
ARBITER
TEMPO
LIFE

JOHN DERIAN COMPANY
6 EAST 2ND STREET
NEW YORK, NY 1003

+1 (212) 677 3917 | Instagram: @johnderiancompany | johnderian.com

But it's Derian's own line of découpage paperweights, plates and trays with images from 18th- and 19th-century nature catalogues and ephemera that are the shop's signature.

Coming Soon is the delightfully eccentric brainchild of owners Fabiana Faria and Helena Barquet, who use their curatorial eye to astutely stock handmade ceramics, colorful carpets, vintage furniture and home goods. Terrazzo planters, pastel milk glass cups, incense and cheeky jewel-toned objects are all here for those with a contemporary aesthetic. T.M.

COMING SOON
53 CANAL STREET
NEW YORK, NY 10002

+1 (212) 226 4548 | Instagram: @comingsoonny | comingsoonnewyork.com

HOW TO HACK
BEING A TOURIST

- It's a myth that New Yorkers aren't friendly. Don't be afraid to ask for directions.
- Look up! So much of the city towers above us. Don't get stuck with your nose in your phone.
- Visit the Metropolitan Museum of Art at night. It's open until 9pm on Fridays and Saturdays ... and prioritize the Egyptian wing.
- The Guggenheim Museum is open until 8pm Saturday through Tuesday and is free from 5pm to 7.30pm on Saturdays.
- The art galleries in Chelsea are closed on Sundays and Mondays.
- If you must go to the top of the Empire State Building, go *after* dinner. The City That Never Sleeps' sparkles brightest at night and the last elevator up is at 1.15am, 365 days a year.

- Skip a visit to the Statue of Liberty in favor of a boat ride in the New York harbor from which you can get a great view of Our Lady and of the city. An ideal destination is the LMCC's Arts Center, the new contemporary studio and exhibition space on Governors Island, which is open seasonally and accessible by ferry.
- Ferries are our friends: water taxis connect the boroughs, give respite from the bustle of mass transportation and there's never any traffic.
- Yoga for the People offers $10 classes.
- Eat at our best restaurants at lunchtime (Le Bernardin, Cosme, Casa Mono ...)
- Citibikes are great. Stay in your lane and don't go against the traffic.
- At Grand Central Station, look up at the constellations on the Beaux-Arts ceiling. In the northwest corner of the dome, you'll see a darker square, which was left after the ceiling was cleaned to show patrons the damage a century of soot had done.

T.M.

MINETTA
TAVERN
RESTAURANT
ONE WAY
WHA?
LANDMARK

#11

ICONIC PLACES. NOT SECRET. **JUST UNMISSABLE**

> Minetta Tavern, a great New York classic

This is everything you'd want from a great New York classic. With its red booth seating, dark wood and late-evening lighting, this 1930s gem has long been associated with the neighborhood's literary life (Hemingway was said to be a regular). Relaunched in 2009 with a chic and timeless tavern spirit, it draws crowds for its old-school atmosphere and a quality menu that won't disappoint. The Black Label Burger has become something of a house classic and is regarded as "legendary' by New Yorkers.

> The Grill, the ultra-exclusive restaurant

This restaurant was designed in 1958 by the celebrated German-born American architect Mies van der Rohe. What makes The Grill truly special is the ritual of it all: impeccable service, dishes prepared and finished at the table, and a proudly American menu of timeless classics including prime rib, house crab cake, impressive cuts of meat, and perfectly mixed cocktails. The whole experience has a wonderful "Mad Men" feel to it.

MINETTA TAVERN
113 MACDOUGAL STREET
NEW YORK, NY 10012

+1 (212) 475 3850 | Instagram: @minettatavernny | minettatavernny.com

THE GRILL
THE SEAGRAM BUILDING
99 EAST 52ND STREET
NEW YORK, NY 10022

+1 (212) 375 9001 | Instagram: @thegrillny | thegrillnewyork.com

> The Odeon, the then, now, & hopefully forever NYC restaurant

In 1980, three restaurateurs – brothers Keith and Brian McNally and Lynn Wagenknecht – who would each go on to open some of the city's most beloved eateries and watering holes, conceived of New York's perfect brasserie in a former 1930s cafeteria. Frequented by creatives (Basquiat, Warhol, Calvin Klein, Madonna and DeNiro, to name a few) and memorialized in Jay McInerney's Bright Lights, Big City, The Odeon defined a cocaine-fueled era of excess. Though the vibe has mellowed considerably, the restaurant remains a beacon of our city that's flourished through fads and floods. With something for everyone on the menu, it's less a place for tourists than a neighborhood anchor and destination for true New Yorkers. Let's hope we can visit for another forty years. T.M.

THE ODEON
145 WEST BROADWAY
NEW YORK, NY 10013

+1 (212) 2330 507

theodeonrestaurant.com

© THE ODEON

> Katz's Delicatessen, the best pastrami sandwich

The drooling begins when we enter Katz's and get our little orange ticket. It's anticipation for the pastrami on rye that we're about to demolish, but it's also for the atmosphere, the energy, the simple joy.

Since it opened in 1888, Katz's has provided great food and a welcoming environment to its community. In the late 19th century, when Jewish immigrants made New York City the Yiddish theater capital of the world, Katz's became their de facto clubhouse and meeting spot. It's been beloved by celebrities ever since (attested to by the kitschy photos on the walls), but it's Katz's authenticity and consistency that have made it endure for New Yorkers.

PRO TIP: The order is simple: pastrami with mustard on rye. It comes with blissfully snappy pickles and while we're at it, we like the coleslaw.

T.M.

KATZ'S DELICATESSEN
205 EAST HOUSTON STREET
(CORNER OF LUDLOW STREET)
NEW YORK, NY 10002

+1 (212) 254 2246	Instagram: @katzdeli	katzsdelicatessen.com

KATZ'S
KATZ'S DELICATESSEN
Marshalls
NOW OPEN
Ludlow St
WAY

CATERED
DELIVERED
1-800-4-HOT-DOG

KATZ'S DELICATESSEN
205 EAST HOUSTON STREET
ESTABLISHED 1888
Send A Salami To Your Boy In The Army
SELTZER
(800) 4 HOT DOG

- SYLVIA WEINSTOCK -

LIFE LESSONS FROM A NATIVE NEW YORKER AND EXTRAORDINARY BAKER, SHORTLY BEFORE HER DEATH IN NOVEMBER 2021.

Where did you grow up?

I grew up in Williamsburg on North 8th Street and Bedford Avenue in a cold-water railroad flat, with no steam heat. I left when I was 19 and got married. I never go back ... Except the other night, I went to Williamsburg for dinner at the Wythe Hotel. I almost stopped to see the corner of North 8th and Bedford, but I don't believe in going backwards, I believe in going forward, so I didn't stop. That chapter is over. That's a good trick: learning how to move on.

I like being older, I get away with a lot of nonsense

For how long have you resided in Tribeca?

I've been living in Tribeca since 1983, and I'm not leaving. If I leave, they carry me out of here!

What's your New York like? Your Tribeca?

The city is divided in many ways. There's the Upper East Side, where the sidewalks are nice and smooth, and everyone lives in tall apartment houses and nobody knows each other. Downtown is another story. In this neighborhood, everyone talks to each other on the street, on the elevator. I had an accident about two years ago and was walking with a cane. People would say, "Can I help you cross the street?" "Can I carry that package for you?" I find this area comforting. People absorb each other and help each other. They pick each other up. They say: "I like your coat!"

How has Tribeca changed in your tenure?
These Tribeca lofts were all factories. Then the artists moved here and lived in 5,000 sq. ft lofts for $20 a month rent. Then the owners found that they could get more money, so goodbye, artists! Now you have people paying $15,000 a month rent. Now these lofts are full of young families.

Where do you like to eat?
I eat at home. I cook for chefs – simple stuff, but they are happy to eat in a home and not in a restaurant. I eat nearby as much as I can because I want to support my neighborhood. I go to Odeon, Frenchette, Petrarca. I went to Tamarind the other day. Years ago as a student, you could get a 3-course meal for $1.95. Life was different. There's nothing like nickels anymore.

What was your profession?
I had Sylvia Weinstock Cakes for 40 years and I had an extraordinary run of clientele.

A lot of out-of-towners find New York City extremely intense. What do you say to them?
New York is a high-energy city ... not stressful. It depends on your attitude. The way people walk, the way they talk ... you feel it. We are a liberal city: tattoos up the gazoo that would not function in the Midwest. That's why they left and came here! They gravitate to an area that's accepting and secondly that's exciting.

Is New York still exciting?
Exciting comes from the people you know and your attitude. You could sit in a wheelchair in the corner and prepare to die. Or you can get out there and go to lunch and talk to young people and learn about them ... People are wonderful. Living here is invigorating.

T.M.

© ALIX PIORUN

#12

ONE OF NEW YORK'S **BEST SPEAKEASIES**

On 7th Avenue, by a pool adorned with a Keith Haring mural, the small triangular building with an utterly unremarkable brown door is the discreet hideout of Little Branch.

Ring the bell and a long staircase leads down to a basement bar that feels frozen in the 1920s: worn leather banquettes, a rippled ceiling, an old cash register, black-and-white photographs... It is easy to picture what the real speakeasies of the era must have been like: not an opulent temple devoted to alcohol, but a modest cellar where the owner could drink with a few trusted friends.

The menu is short but flawlessly executed: classics made with precision, using fresh juices and quality spirits, drawn from historical recipes. Don't hesitate to ask the bartender for guidance. They'll steer you toward what suits your tastes and cravings.

LITTLE BRANCH
20-22 7TH AVENUE SOUTH
NEW YORK, NY 10014

Instagram: @lbbarnyc

#13

THE SECRET SPOT FROM WHERE YOU CAN SEE **NEW YORK'S CRAZIEST BUILDING**

Designed by Julian Schnabel, Palazzo Chupi is probably the craziest building in New York City. It was built in Greenwich Village atop a disused early 20th-century factory and looks as though a Venetian palazzo has been picked up and plonked down here almost by chance. With its pink facade and 180 windows – some adorned with balconies – it's an artist's dream made real, a magnificently whimsical baroque gesture in a city that usually prefers brick and polished glass.

Schnabel oversaw the sumptuous interiors himself: carved fireplaces, Moroccan tilework, exposed-beam ceilings, countless artworks and a 40-ft. swimming pool in the basement.

The best view of Palazzo Chupi is from the rooftop of Westbeth Artists Housing. Here's the trick: walk in as though you're a regular, take the lift to the top floor and head up to the roof – access is usually free. From up there, the view is extraordinary: you can see across the West Village, out to the Hudson and over several historic buildings, including Palazzo Chupi.

PALAZZO CHUPI
360 WEST 11TH STREET
WEST VILLAGE, NEW YORK, NY 10014

Not open to the public

#14

AN ARCHITECTURAL CRUISE AROUND MANHATTAN

Manhattan's vast scale and towering skyline make it impossible to fully appreciate it from street level. Take to the water instead: that's where the perspective truly opens up. A three-hour cruise with the American Institute of Architects circles the entire island, revealing how Manhattan has evolved over the decades. In partnership with Harbor Lines, AIA architects guide you through the city's architectural story, turning a boat trip into an insightful journey through living history.

'AROUND MANHATTAN ARCHITECTURE' CRUISE
DEPARTURE POINT: CHELSEA PIERS (PIER 62)
NEW YORK, NY 10011

+1 (212) 683 0023	Duration: 2 hrs. 45 mins Between $88 and $128	Booking: aiany.org/architecture/tours/boat-tours info@aiany.org

PHOTOS © DENNIS CAHLO

© DENNIS CAHLO

The yachts depart from Chelsea Piers, a location that alone illustrates the evolution of New York's waterfront. Once upon a time, the piers housed a bustling port of docks, gangways and machinery (some relics still remain) used for loading ships. Today, as part of a vast urban regeneration program, they house an enormous sports complex.

Travelling up the Hudson, the city's defining lines emerge: the almost futuristic dominance of the Freedom Tower, the noble solitude of the Empire State Building, then the sudden appearance of Riverside Park around 72nd Street, an island of greenery where residential towers give way to forest.

The slower pace allows you to notice the details: balconies, window frames and ornaments that reveal a style, an era or an architectural firm's signature. You'll also discover the city's inner workings: the iconic water tanks perched on rooftops, and the history and mechanics of the bridges ... from the swing bridge at Spuyten Duyvil, which alternates between ships and trains, to the vertical lift bridge of the Triborough.

This cruise offers an alternative way to discover New York. Rather than rushing past as a hurried spectator, you become a privileged observer aboard a magnificent yacht. Seen from the water, the city reveals its extraordinary scale and genius. An essential experience for anyone wanting to understand Manhattan differently!

THE ICONIC **ARCHITECTURE**

THE BROOKLYN BRIDGE

THE UNITED NATIONS

THE GUGGENHEIM MUSEUM

THE OCULUS

THE CHRYSLER BUILDING

THE EMPIRE STATE BUILDING

15

STARGAZING …
FROM THE HIGH LINE

No need to leave Manhattan to see the stars. Throughout the city, telescopes from the Amateur Astronomers Association are popping up on building rooftops and in parks – at Carl Schurz Park, on Little Island, perched on the High Line, at Lincoln Center, on the Greenpoint Library rooftop and at Evergreens Cemetery, to name but a few.

Even with all of New York's bright lights, you can still catch some amazing views: Saturn's rings, Venus, the Moon's craters. These free sessions are open to everyone, and association members are on hand, happy to share their knowledge. That's when things get really special!

AMATEUR ASTRONOMERS ASSOCIATION

Free events, open to all; booking required

Dates and observation points at: aaa.org
Instagram: @aaadotorg

#16

EXPERIENCE **AN AI MASSAGE**

Fancy stepping into a futuristic world? Head to Remedy Place, a "social wellness club" painted entirely in gray – a color symbolizing balance.

Here you won't find treadmills or weight machines, but cutting-edge equipment like cryogenic and hyperbaric chambers, ice baths, and vitamin infusion rooms.

The best treatment to try: the AI massage. After changing into appropriate clothing, a robotic bed with two arms scans your body to create a bespoke program. An hour of compressions will relieve knots and sore muscles in the shoulders and back, and the integrated screen allows you to adjust the pressure, skip a movement or linger longer on a particularly tight spot.

Nothing will ever replace a therapist's touch, but the technical prowess of this massage is well worth experiencing.

REMEDY PLACE FLATIRON
12 WEST 21ST STREET
NEW YORK, NY 10010
+1 (917) 727 7950

REMEDY PLACE SOHO
11 GREENE STREET
NEW YORK, NY 10013
+1 (212) 201 5707

One-hour massage: $160

Instagram: @remedyplace

remedyplace.com

© BENJAMIN HOLTROP

© REMEDY PLACE

© REMEDY PLACE

© REMEDY PLACE

#17

PLAY TENNIS **IN A 107-YEAR-OLD TRAIN STATION**

It's essential to visit Grand Central Station, the exquisite Beaux-Arts midtown wonder of architecture and engineering. Admire its reverse Zodiac dome and hunt for its mysterious whisper chamber, but then, why not go play tennis on the little-known courts on the 4th floor?

The Vanderbilt Tennis Club resides in a space that from the 1920s to the 1950s was home to the Grand Central Art Galleries, founded by painter John Singer Sargent among others. Now there are two courts (one regulation size, one junior) on which anyone can play.

T.M.

VANDERBILT TENNIS CLUB
15 VANDERBILT AVE (4TH FLOOR)
NEW YORK, NY 10017

+1 (212) 599 6500
Reservations only

vanderbilttennisclub.com

BEMELMANS BAR
THE CARLYLE (ENTRANCE ON MADISON AVENUE)
35 EAST 76TH STREET
NEW YORK, NY 10021

+1 (212) 744 1600

rosewoodhotels.com/en/the-carlyle-new-york/dining/bemelmans-bar
Instagram: @rosewoodthecarlyle

#18

ENJOY AN APERITIF **IN FRONT OF LUDWIG BEMELMANS' MURALS**

There's a pang of anticipation every time we enter Bemelmans, the illustrious Art Deco bar at the Carlyle Hotel with the only remaining public murals by Ludwig Bemelmans, illustrator of the *Madeline* children's books.

Will the waiter procure us a table? Who will we run into?

Soon we've taken a sip of a mammoth martini and our hearts flutter with anticipation as the pianist sits and begins to play. We like to be here just as he arrives (5.30pm, daily) so that we can experience this private thrill. As the music and drink take effect, we observe our surroundings: preppy Upper East Siders, socialites with plastic faces, dignitaries and an occasional celebrity or strumpet. There's laughter, chatter and the tinkling of glasses, but most importantly, the songs reverberating off the storied golden walls.

T.M.

EXIT
BANKER

#19

A KOSHER DELI **HIDING A COCKTAIL BAR**

Delicatessen and restaurant: the Second Ave Deli has been serving New Yorkers certified kosher Jewish products since 1954. And since 2017, the 2nd Floor Bar & Essen (which means "eat" in Yiddish) has been serving refined "tapas" versions of their products too.

Look for the separate entrance on East 75th Street between 1st Avenue and York Avenue and head upstairs for deviled eggs, mini pastrami burgers and *gefilte* fish croquettes with horseradish. The cocktail menu takes inspiration from Jewish culinary traditions, with drinks like the Upper Eastsider (a refined twist on the Moscow mule) alongside kosher-certified espresso martinis and piña coladas.

THE 2ND FLOOR
1442 1ST AVENUE (2ND FLOOR)
UPPER EAST SIDE
NEW YORK, NY 10021

Thursday, Friday and Saturday evenings	+1 (212) 737 1700	2ndfloor.com Instagram: @2ndavedeli

© MELISSA HOM

© ALIX PIORUN

© DANIELLE ADAMS

ELOVED SON HEAR HI
FRIDAY

#20

HAVE YOUR BIKE BLESSED

New York's streets can be perilous for cyclists. A brilliant solution: head to the Cathedral of St. John the Divine to have your bike blessed (and therefore protected).

Launched in 1998 by Glen Goldstein, this open-to-all event attracts growing crowds each May. Led by three bagpipers, hundreds of cyclists wheel their bikes under the cathedral porch and into the central aisle, where they line up in rows in a cheerful atmosphere. From his podium, the Reverend delivers the blessing: "Whether you cycle to relax or to get to work, whatever reason drives you to ride without the aid of an engine, you're doing a good thing."

After the sermon, cyclists ring their bells, delighted to set off with peace of mind. New York's streets are now that bit safer.

Not to be missed if you're in New York in May.

FREE

Find the next date at: stjohndivine.org or theblessingofthebikes.com

Sylvia's

#21

A MARVELOUS MORNING **IN HARLEM**

Let's be real: there is no soul of New York without Harlem and a trip to New York City is incomplete without a visit. The best day to head uptown is Thursday. Make sure to visit the Studio Museum of Harlem, showcasing work by artists of African descent, and the Schomberg Center for Research in Black Culture, in between visits to Harlem's iconic restaurants.

Sylvia's, the famous eatery that's been serving soul food since 1962, is an institution (don't skip a side of the buttery grits), and next-door Red Rooster Harlem, chef Marcus Samuellson's bustling ode to the neighborhood's diverse culinary traditions, is boisterous and fun.

SYLVIA'S
328 MALCOLM X BOULEVARD
NEW YORK, NY 10027

+1 (212) 996 0660 | Instagram: @sylviasrestaurant | sylviasrestaurant.com

CHARLES PAN FRIED CHICKEN
340 WEST 145 STREET
(AT THE CORNER OF EDGECOME AVENUE)
NEW YORK, NY 10039

+1 (212) 281 1800

Instagram:
@charlespanfriedchicken

charlespanfriedchicken.com

But most importantly, visit Charles' Country Pan Fried Chicken, the informal joint in its new location on West 145th Street. Born on a plantation in the South and a New Yorker since 1965, owner Charles Gabriel makes the best fried chicken we've ever tasted. Walk off the sweet potato (obligatory side) stupor by strolling south, past the Apollo Theater and Hotel Theresa, to Harlem Haberdashery to browse their signature clothing line. T.M.

#22

ENJOY CLASSICAL MUSIC **IN THE CITY'S SECRET CRYPTS**

Who says classical music can only be performed in formal concert halls and drab recital spaces? Certainly not Andrew Ousley, who since 2015 has been organizing performances in the city's rarely accessed and even less frequently utilized crypts and catacombs. Through his nonprofit Death of Classical, Ousley has put on interpretive dance performances among the tombs of Brooklyn's Green-Wood Cemetery and produced opera under the vaulted masonry beneath Harlem's Church of the Intercession.

DEATH OF CLASSICAL
There are three main venues
deathofclassical.com
Instagram: @deathofclassical

OR

The Crypt under the Church of the Intercession (550 West 155th Street New York, NY 10032)	The Green-Wood Cemetery and Catacombs (500 25th Street Brooklyn, NY 11232)	The Crypt under the Cathedral of St. John the Divine (1047 Amsterdam Avenue New York, NY 10025)

© KEVIN CONDON

The son of an amateur opera singer and an Episcopal priest, Ousley believes that by presenting these shows in unique settings he can bring newfound excitement to age-old traditions.

And judging by Death of Classical's exponential growth and success in its decade of existence, he's onto something.

These performances are not for the faint of heart – the spaces often feel alive with both death and spirits, and the content is generally dark and haunting – but patrons are not only rewarded with access to these exclusive, subterranean corners of the city but also take home memories of them coming alive with song, if only for one night.

© KEVIN CONDON

© STEVEN PISANO

#23

A SECRET JAPANESE BAR HIDDEN AT THE BACK OF A BISTRO

To reach Karasu, walk through Walter's and head to the black door at the back that barely stands out against the decor. Keep your eyes out in the bustling bistro as the door is almost invisible. On the other side, the atmosphere shifts completely: soft lighting, hushed surroundings – you lose track of time, and that's exactly the point!

Karasu ("little crow' in Japanese) is more than just a Japanese whisky bar. The place stands out for its exceptional culinary approach. All the dishes are designed for sharing and built around the concept of *washoku*, a culinary philosophy that seeks balance throughout the meal. Each dish brings different flavors, textures and colors into balance. Among the must-tries are the Ikura Don and the cauliflower steak with shiso sauce.

KARASU
166 DEKALB AVENUE
BROOKLYN, NY 11217

Open every evening

+1 (347) 542 8627

karasubk.com
Instagram: @karasubk

© ALIX PIORUN

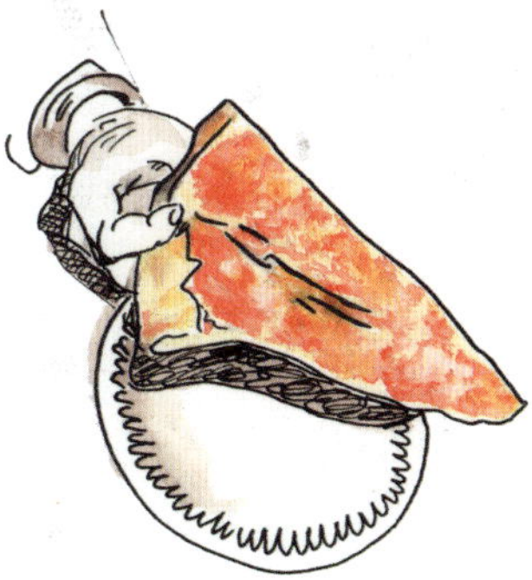

#24

EVERLASTING **PIZZA PARTY**

We are a pizza town. We've got slice shops aplenty and fancy pizza galore – but there's nowhere quite like Roberta's, the Bushwick restaurant that defines the hipster artists' community from which it grew. At graffiti-covered Roberta's, the woodfire glows onto the picnic tables. It's some of the best pizza and rustic Italian fare one can hope to find, and has a tiki bar and ramshackle garden, to boot. Twelve years in, Roberta's has a 2-Michelin-star restaurant, Blanca, across its back garden and their frozen pies are sold in grocery stores nationwide. Still, eating *morcilla* with pear and a "Cowabunga Dude" pizza while listening to rock in their rough and tumble dining room is singular to this original spot and cannot be recreated in the privacy of your own home.

T.M.

ROBERTA'S
261 MOORE STREET
BROOKLYN, NY 11206

+1 (718) 417 1118 | Instagram: @robestaspizza | robertaspizza.com

Dull

HOW TO EAT A NEW YORK SLICE

Slice shops, as we New Yorkers fondly call them, are as prevalent and essential to us as our delis: there's pretty much one on every block and they're a cornerstone of New Yorkers' diets, particularly for our late-night rebel rousers. Perfect for a disco dinner before a night of revelry, perfect for an essential snack after a night of drinking, and perfectly adequate for breakfast the next day, our slices are the best way to survive on a budget in this exorbitant metropolis.

But if you want to blend in with the locals, this is how you should master your slice:

(Note: this is a point of controversy.) T.M.

#25

WILLIAMSBURG **PUNCH LIST**

If you want to stay in Brooklyn, there's nowhere better than the Wythe, the original Williamsburg hotel in a converted 117-year-old factory building. You don't have to be a guest to enjoy its two restaurant-bars, Lemon's and Le Crocodile, but with their excellent food and sexy scenes, they help to make the Wythe a heavenly place to rest your head.

Time spent in Williamsburg must include a drink and a snack at Achilles Heel in Greenpoint, one of the world's most perfect bars. Have a steam, sauna and massage at Bathhouse. Scavenge at vintage emporium Beacon's Closet. The stylish Mociun promises a sophisticated shopping experience featuring curated jewelry and exquisite home goods. Catch an unusual musical show in a one-of-a-kind structure at National Sawdust or a concert at the Union Pool. Book ahead for dinner at exceptional Italian, Lilia (get the *Mafaldini*!), or Michelin-starred natural wine bar, The Four Horsemen (also a fantastic place for lunch). No reservations? Head to Diner, the restaurant that was here before all the rest. Still raring to go? Hit Baby's All Right for live music and frisky vibes.

T.M.

WYTHE HOTEL
80 WYTHE AVENUE
BROOKLYN, NY 11249

+1 (718) 460 8000	Instagram: @wythehotel	wythehotel.com

WYTHE HOTEL

WYTHE HOTEL

NATIONAL SAWDUST
80 NORTH 6TH STREET
BROOKLYN, NY 11249

+1 (646) 779 8455 | Instagram: @nationalsawdust | nationalsawdust.org

© VICENTE MUÑOZ

© EVAN SUNG

LILIA
567 UNION AVENUE
BROOKLYN, NY 11211

Instagram: @lilianewyork

BATHHOUSE ▲
103 NORTH 10TH STREET
BROOKLYN, NY 11249

+1 (929) 489 2284	Instagram: @bathhouse	abathhouse.com

MOCIUN
683 DRIGGS AVENUE
BROOKLYN, NY 11211

+1 (347) 227 8966	Instagram: @mociun	mociun.com

© NICHOLAS CALCOTT

MOCIUN

#26

A NEW-GENERATION SAUNA

What if modern business meetings were held in swimwear? That's precisely what's happening in Othership, a 6,460-sq.-ft. space in the heart of Williamsburg, Brooklyn.

The 75-minute experience – somewhere between a Cirque du Soleil show and group therapy – begins in a communal room. "Journeyers' drink beneficial herbal teas before following their guide into a sauna heated to 85°C/185°F.

What follows is a meticulously choreographed routine combining deep breathing exercises, throwing balls of essential oils, and creating smoke effects on hot stones for theatrical impact.

Following a refreshing visit to the communal showers, the group then moves to a cold room equipped with six baths ranging from 0–4°C/32–40°F. The challenge: 3 minutes of immersion before the gong sounds, signaling it's time to head back for round two. According to theory, the cold is said to help break down emotional barriers, fostering deeper connections between participants.

OTHERSHIP
25 KENT AVENUE
BROOKLYN, NY 11249

+1 (212) 871-4505

othership.us
Instagram: @othership

75-min. session: $64

DEXTER
STACK DRYER
EXPRESS
DRYER
EXPRESS
SPACE SHUTTLE
17
18

#27

NOT YOUR AVERAGE **LAUNDERETTE**

The less observant might think this is a perfectly ordinary launderette, despite the unexpected presence of a few pinball machines and dog portraits. After all, the main room is full of working washing machines and tumble dryers. But look more closely at the two dryers at the back and you'll spot something else entirely through their portholes: a hidden room with no washing machines at all, just a bar and an impressive collection of pinball games.

You'll also meet an animatronic chimp who tells fortunes and dispenses beer in exchange for a few coins. Board games, skee-ball and plenty more round out the experience. People rarely leave Sunshine Laundromat with clean clothes, but they almost always leave smiling!

SUNSHINE LAUNDROMAT
860 MANHATTAN AVENUE
BROOKLYN, NY 11222

+1 (718) 475 2055 | Instagram: @sunshinelaundromat | sunshinelaundromat.com

© ALAMY / RICHARD LEVINE

#28

A BUCOLIC WATERWAY **IN THE HEART OF THE BRONX**

Narrow and barely 24 miles long, the Bronx River flows through the heart of the borough of the same name. Less than 330 feet from the elevated train that runs above the Bronx, concrete and tarmac give way to scenery as idyllic as it is unexpected: along the tree-lined riverbanks, rabbits frolic alongside numerous bird species and beavers. Having vanished two centuries ago (the fur of these rodents was the primary source of income for the early colonies), they returned to the river's waters a few years ago.

Whilst it's pleasant to stroll along the banks, the best way to appreciate the river is undoubtedly by canoe.

As well as working to preserve this enchanting setting, the Bronx River Alliance offers various options for exploring the river by canoe. You can paddle free of charge along a short stretch, or for a modest sum, embark on a proper expedition: long stretches through woodland give way to industrial buildings, all the way to Long Island Sound.

The hardest part for anyone who has discovered this enchanting spot is convincing other New Yorkers that it actually exists...

BRONX RIVER ALLIANCE

Schedule of outings: bronxriver.org

Free paddling during summer
Paid private excursions

NOGUCHI MUSEUM
9-01 33RD ROAD (AT VERNON BOULEVARD)
LONG ISLAND CITY, NY 11106

+1 (718) 204 7088	Instagram: @noguchimuseum	noguchi.org

HOW TO CONQUER **QUEENS**

There are so many reasons to fall in love with Queens. Twenty minutes from Midtown Manhattan, in Long Island City, MoMA PS1 is one of America's largest institutions dedicated to contemporary art. But for a tactile, serene and captivating experience, nothing compares to the Isamu Noguchi Foundation and Garden Museum, where there are rarely crowds and you can walk among the pioneering Japanese artist-designer's works in stone, wood, brass and, of course, paper.

Do not leave Queens without eating. Jackson Heights is one of the most multicultural experiences in the world, let alone New York City. There are approximately 6,000 restaurants in Queens (emblematic of the 120 nationalities that reside in this borough) and Little India' (74th Street off Roosevelt Avenue) has a particularly diverse selection. Follow a passageway between two cellphone shops to unassuming Lhasa Fast Food for beef and chive *momos* (South Asian dumplings) and myriad other spicy Tibetan delights.

MOMA PS1
22–25 JACKSON AVENUE
QUEENS, NY 11101

+1 (718) 784 2086 | Instagram: @momaps1 | moma.org/ps1

LHASA FRESH FOOD
76-03 37TH AVENUE
JACKSON HEIGHTS, NY 11372

+1 (917) 745 0364

But the essence of what we love about eating in New York is at Dawa's in Woodside, where chef Dawa Bhuti combines her Himalayan heritage with the impeccable sourcing ethos she learned while cooking at upscale NYC restaurants. T.M.

DAWA'S
51-18 SKILLMAN AVENUE
WOODSIDE, NY 11377

+1 (718) 899 8629	Instagram: @dawasnyc	dawasnyc.com

SUSHI ON ME

#30

A WILD EXPERIENCE

In an unglamorous corner of Queens where Jackson Heights meets Elmhurst, tucked beneath the elevated subway tracks across from a takeaway shop, that's where you'll find the entrance of Sushi On Me.

Once you're inside, things get wonderfully chaotic. Sake flows abundantly, the chefs put on a show, flamethrowers make an appearance, shots keep coming, everyone's singing, and superb sashimi and nigiri arrive piece by piece.

Not keen on venturing that far? A Sushi On Me has also opened in Williamsburg, with an 18-course Thai and Japanese tasting menu for $129 (90 minutes). But the original restaurant's experience is one of a kind.

SUSHI ON ME
71–26 ROOSEVELT AVENUE (BASEMENT)
ELMHURST, NY 11372

Reservations: reservation.sushionme@gmail.com or text +1 (929) 821 5598	$89 menu (60-min. slot) Cash only	Instagram: @sushionme.nyc

Rockaway Beach
Atlantic Ocean
Cross Bay Bridge
TACOWAY BEACH
CHANNEL DR.
ROCKAWAY
BEACH
BLVD.
SHORE FRONT
PKWY
BEACH
102 ND
94TH
77TH
73RD
67 TH
59TH ST.
walk up beach
1
2
3
4
5
6
7
8
9
10
11
12
13

#31

NEW YORK CITY'S **VERY OWN SURF TOWN**

Our very own beachtown, the Far Rockaways are a car or subway (a train) ride away. We asked local couple, Anna Polonsky (founder of branding studio Polonsky & Friends) and Fernando Aciar (ceramicist and creator of OStudio), to show us how to Rockaway like pros:

Come to the beach! It's beautiful even in winter!

1. For a great walk, start at Beach 67 and work your way up.

2. Uma's – delicious Uzbeki food!
92-07 Rockaway Beach Blvd

3. Tacoway Beach* – the spot that made Rockaway famous!
Surf Club, 302 Beach 87th St

4. La Cevicheria* – best in town!
97-01 Shore Front Pkwy, Beach 97th St

*Open seasonally

5. Goody's – top-notch Jamaican food!
7018 Amstel Blvd, Arverne

6. Rippers* – classic burger & rock n' roll!
8601 Shore Front Pkwy, Beach 86th St

7. Rockaway Brewing Co. – local beer + cool rotating food vendors & fun events, etc.
415 B 72nd St, Arverne

8. Rockaway Beach Bakery – don't miss their ham & cheese croissants and brownies!
87-10 Rockaway Beach Blvd

9. Cuisine by Claudette – we love the banana bread and Açaí bowls!
190 Beach 69th St, Arverne

10. Caracas* – best *arepas* in town!
106-01 Shore Front Pkwy

11.a. Edgemere Farm* – organic produce, honey and groceries!
385 B 45th St

11.b. Edgemere Weekend Market Stand – year-round!
3-23 Beach 74th St, Far Rockaway, NY 11692

12. Marina on 72 offers boat rides on bay (go at sunset!)

13. The Castle Rockaway – rooms to rent, events, pop ups, workshops ++!
Beach 117th St

T.M.

*Open seasonally

MANY THANKS TO

Acknowledgments from Tarajia Morrell:

FANY PÉCHIODAT for giving me the opportunity to fall in love with my hometown all over again.

LIZ BARCLAY AND ABBIE ZUIDEMA for their persistence, generosity and gorgeous imagery that make this book come to life.

THOMAS JONGLEZ for his contemporary take on guidebooks for inquisitive, modern travelers.

EMILIEN CRESPO for the songs, and for suggesting me to Fany and encouraging me to share my New York.

ANNA POLONSKY AND FERNANDO ACIAR for the introductions they make for me to foodies and friends all over the world and for sharing their contribution herein.

NASTASSIA LOPEZ for listening, reading, guidance and friendship.

ADAM PLATT for making me laugh and consider how essential restaurants are to life, even years before we ever met.

SYLVIA WEINSTOCK for sharing her sage wisdom and contagious zeal for life.

MAMA CATHY MORRELL for her support and keen editorial eye.

PAPA PETER MORRELL for showing me how to love restaurants, from diners to fine dining, from Day One.

This book was created by:
Tarajia Morrell (T.M.), Marine Sanclemente and Hannah Frishberg, texts
Liz Barclay, photographs (unless otherwise stated)
Abbie Zuidema, illustrations
Emmanuelle Willard Toulemonde, layout
Jana Gough, editing
Olivia Fuller, translation
Susan R. Pollack, proofreading
Mado de La Quintinie, publishing

Cover photo: © Adobe Stock / Maridav

You can write to us at info@jonglezpublishing.com
Follow us on Instagram: @jonglez_publishing

THANK YOU

STOP
ONE WAY
NO PARKING ANYTIME

ONE WAY
ALL TRAFFIC
ONE WAY
STOP
ONE WAY

From the same publisher

Photo Books

Abandoned America: The age of Consequences
Abandoned Asylums
Abandoned Australia
Abandoned Belgium
Abandoned Churches: Unclaimed Places of Worship
Abandoned Cinemas of the World
Abandoned France
Abandoned Germany
Abandoned Lebanon
Abandoned Italy
Abandoned Japan
Abandoned Spain
Abandoned USSR
Abandoned World – An AI-generated exploration
After the Final Curtain: The Fall of the American Movie Theater
After the Final Curtain: America's Abandoned Theaters
Baikonur – Vestiges of the Soviet Space Program
Cinemas – A French Heritage
Chernobyl's Atomic Legacy – 25 years after disaster
Clickbait – A visual journey through AI-generated stories
Destination: Wellness – Our 35 best places in the world to take time out
Forbidden Places – Exploring our Abandoned Heritage
Forgotten Heritage
Oblivion
Parisian Theatres – Exceptional Venues
Secret Art Nouveau
Secret Sacred Sites
The cinemas of India – An exceptional heritage
Venice deserted
Venice from the skies

"Confidential" and "Soul of" Guides

Berlin Confidential
Lisbon Confidential
Los Angeles Confidential
Malta Confidential
Marrakesh Confidential
Munich Confidential
Paris Confidential

Soul of Amsterdam - A guide to the 30 best experiences
Soul of Athens – 30 experiences
Soul of Barcelona – 30 experiences
Soul of Brussels – A guide to exceptional experiences
Soul of Detroit – A guide to exceptional experiences
Soul of Kyoto – A guide to exceptional experiences
Soul of Marseille – A guide to exceptional experiences
Soul of Milan – A guide to exceptional experiences
Soul of Rome – A guide to exceptional experiences
Soul of Tokyo – A guide to exceptional experiences
Soul of Venice – A guide to exceptional experiences
Soul of Vienna – A guide to exceptional experiences

Atlases of curiosities

Atlas of extreme weather
Atlas of forbidden places
Atlas of geographical curiosities
Atlas of geographical curiosities – Britain
Atlas of unusual wines
Atlas of urban vineyards

Secret atlases

Berlin – The secret atlas
London – The secret atlas
New York – The secret atlas
Paris – The secret atlas
Rome – The secret atlas
Venice – The secret atlas

"Secret" Guides

Secret Amsterdam
Secret Bali – An unusual guide
Secret Bangkok
Secret Barcelona
Secret Bars & Restaurants in Paris
Secret Bath – An unusual guide
Secret Belfast
Secret Berlin
Secret Boston – An unusual guide
Secret Brighton – An unusual guide
Secret Brooklyn
Secret Brussels
Secret Budapest
Secret Buenos Aires
Secret Campania
Secret Cape Town
Secret Copenhagen
Secret Corsica
Secret Dolomites
Secret Dublin – An unusual guide
Secret Edinburgh – An unusual guide
Secret Florence
Secret French Riviera
Secret Geneva
Secret Glasgow – An unusual guide
Secret Granada
Secret Helsinki
Secret Istanbul
Secret Johannesburg
Secret Kuala Lumpur
Secret Lisbon
Secret Liverpool – An unusual guide
Secret London – An unusual guide
Secret London – Unusual Bars & Restaurants
Secret Los Angeles – An unusual guide
Secret Louisiana
Secret Madrid
Secret Mexico City
Secret Milan
Secret Montreal – An unusual guide
Secret Naples
Secret New Orleans – An unusual guide
Secret New York – An unusual guide
Secret New York – Curious Activities
Secret New York – Hidden Bars & Restaurants
Secret Normandy
Secret Paris
Secret Potsdam
Secret Prague
Secret Provence
Secret Rio
Secret Rome
Secret Seville
Secret Singapore
Secret Stockholm
Secret Strasbourg
Secret Sussex – An unusual guide
Secret Tokyo
Secret Tuscany
Secret Venice
Secret Venice Lagoon
Secret Vienna
Secret Washington DC – An unusual guide
Secret York – An unusual guide

Registration of copyright: September 2026 – Edition: 01
ISBN: 978-2-38715-080-6
Printed in June 2026 in Bulgaria by Dedrax